C000005203

WHAT HAPPENED TO THE CINEMA NEAR YOU?

Volume 1: NORFOLK

A Pictorial Survey by Stephen Peart

NORTHACRES

Published to celebrate one hundred years of the cinema in England.

First published in 1996 by Northacres.
4, Beech Drive, Strumpshaw, Norwich NR13 4AF.

© Copyright Stephen Peart 1996

All rights reserved
ISBN 0 9517192 0 3

Typeset and printed by Geo. R. Reeve Ltd.
9-11 Town Green, Wymondham, Norfolk NR18 0BD.

CONTENTS

Front Cover: The Carlton, Norwich – Photographed by George Plunkett.
Back Cover: Odeon, Norwich, during demolition 1971.

ACKNOWLEDGEMENTS

The Author is indebted to everyone who answered questions during the compilation of this book, particularly Colin Aldis, Ken Arnott, Charles Bayfield, Patricia Finch (Swaffham Museum), John Oliver and Philip Yaxley.

Permission to reproduce photographs is credited to the following:-
John Barker, Richard Bond, Mr Checkley, Eric Cooper, Eastern Daily Press, Barry Gibbs, Dorothy Jean, George Jessup, Gail McPhee, John Maltby, Frank Marwood, Mrs Nicholls, George Plunkett, and Gladys Skedge.

THE AUTHOR

Stephen Peart developed a lifelong interest in cinemas after being taken to see the screen adaptation of Anna Sewell's "Black Beauty" at The County, Aylsham in 1948. He researched and wrote "The Picture House in East Anglia" published by Dalton, 1980 and is a member of the Cinema Theatre Association.

PROLOGUE

There was a time when the cinema had its place in each community. Like Church and public house it was within reach of everybody. Today, when advertisements announce a film as "showing at a cinema near you" the journey could be long and against all will.

Norfolk once supported seventy cinemas. Half of them were purpose-built, while the rest had been converted from existing structures. Of those seventy 'picture houses' once spread across the county, seven full time cinemas remain open for business, supporting twenty 'screens' between them, while the remainder have been put to other uses or demolished.

The early cinemas were built for silent films and converted when 'talkies' came in 1929. During the Edwardian period the most popular names were 'Electric', 'Empire', 'Palace' and 'Picture House'. The word 'cinema' took longer to evolve so 'going to the pictures' became the colloquialism.

Architecture reached a peak in luxury during the 1930s when 'super' cinemas were designed and built for sound films. The Electric Palaces were cast aside and a new generation of names appeared like Regal, Carlton, Ritz and Capitol.

A night at the pictures became an occasion and the universal escape from reality as audiences immersed themselves into films and glimpsed lifestyles they could only dream of experiencing. Patrons enjoyed the comforts of a cinema, unknown in their homes, such as fitted carpets and central heating.

The achievements in establishing such places involved feats of business and engineering which have passed with little record. A study of former cinema buildings may reveal some unsightly structures but the atmosphere inside was all that counted. When the lights had dimmed the comedy or tragedy cast on the screen was a universal language in town or village.

When the second war came, even more people went to the cinema. The attendance records were broken but in the aftermath the course of British life changed and brought a decline in the cinema-going habit. The trade regarded 1949 as the year "things went wrong" and by 1956 one in ten cinemas was reported to be losing money. Remarkably, the cinema entrepreneurs of the 1930s were aware their lucrative ventures would not last. One Norwich architect was briefed to design auditoriums which would stand for just 25 years.

An expansion of BBC Television and the launch of ITV brought a rash of closures in the late 1950s and early 1960s. But television can only share the blame along with the proliferation of the motor car and the explosion of consumer spending which split the family budget more ways. Everyone began acquiring products they had once only dreamed of owning, and they grew tired of the cinema.

By the mid 1970s the last closures brought the number of surviving cinemas to its present level. Those enjoying business now are being 'discovered' by a young audience who know little of the past of 'the pictures'. They have a better awareness brought about by the improved distribution of information by newspapers and television.

Recollections of "going to the pictures" prompt amusing stories like "sneaking into a more expensive seat while the usherette's back was turned", "getting in for nothing after a friend inside had opened the fire exit" or "getting into X rated films when under 18". Whatever the story; what happened to the cinema near you?

This pictorial survey concerns registered buildings which appeared or were licensed as a result of the Cinematograph Act 1909, the trade's first Parliamentary Bill.

The dates against each entry in the following pages refer to that cinema's period of operation, followed by a note of its current state: open, demolished or changed to another use.

The frequent reference to "Talkies" or "Talking Pictures" was the common description of sound films when they first appeared in 1929.

ATTLEBOROUGH

CINEMA/REGAL – Exchange Street

1919-1959   Change of Use

This impressive white-brick building of 1863 was once the Town Hall and retains some evidence of its time as Attleborough's cinema. Bricked-up windows, the addition of ventilation outlets and traces of interior decor betray its last use as a 'cinematograph hall'.

The Town Hall became a 'picture theatre' when the Eastern Counties Cinema Company set-up on Wednesdays and Thursdays each week in 1919. Gilbert Wright, a newsagent in Church Street, accompanied the silent films with his upright iron-framed piano. For many years the cinema was under the ownership of Frank Yeates who lived at The Laurels in Queen's Square.

The building was converted to show 'talking pictures' by E. Tofts, the builders, after which the admission prices were increased threefold.

In the 1930s, free tickets were provided for the inmates of the neighbouring Wayland Workhouse on Saturday mornings who would be route-marched the two miles to the cinema. During the war years the Regal was a favourite haunt of American Servicemen stationed at Airfields in the locality.

The Bostock Cinema Circuit acquired the hall in 1938, renaming it The Regal and operated the business in conjunction with their other cinemas around East Anglia until its closure in 1959. The building is now the workshops of A.W. Myhill & Son Ltd.

AYLSHAM

COUNTY – Cawston Road

1937-1960   Change of Use

Aylsham's custom designed County cinema brought to an end the weekly visit of mobile shows in the Town Hall.

The County was a futuristic building for the historic town of Aylsham. It was the bold venture of local businessmen, J.B. Postle, J.F. Bond, Lord Walpole and R. Wolsey who formed the Aylsham Cinema Company under the Managing Directorship of Victor Harrison. Operating as VEH Cinemas, Harrison had established a string of cinemas from the Norfolk Coast to Walton-on-the-Naze, in Essex.

The County's construction was the work of Aylsham's builder, J.W. Palmer, deploying rapid and economic building methods to the plans of Robert Bond, a Norwich architect who was achieving a good reputation for cinema design.

The County was opened on 15th September, 1937 by Lady Walpole of Wolterton when the 'big film' was "Rhodes of Africa" starring Walter Houston.

In 1954 the latest widescreen system Cinemascope was installed at great expense and generated excitement when Victor Harrison secured this latest innovation before it was available in Norwich.

For 23 years the County served Aylsham and surrounding villages but eventually succumbed to dwindling audiences. The cinema was closed in September 1960 after showing its last film "The Best of Everything". The building remained vacant until the following year when Norfolk County Council bought it for £3,150 at a public auction for conversion into a youth centre.

AYLSHAM

West End Cinema – Penfold Street

1921-1924   Change of Use

This short-lived cinema was established in premises of the Norwich Co-op Society. The proprietors were Elkington, Evans & Turner. A notable film shown here in 1922 was the wedding of Princess Mary, King George's daughter. The Norwich Co-op stores was established here in 1924 and after closure the building became the print works of F.C. Barnwell.

Town Hall – Market Place

1921-1937   Normal Use

The Town Hall was a regular venue for films operated by the Eastern Counties Cinematograph Company on Fridays, Saturdays and Mondays in rotation with their shows at Attleborough. Aylsham's first 'talkies' were shown here and continued until the County opened in 1937. There were films twice nightly from 6 o'clock with afternoon performances on Saturdays.

BURNHAM MARKET

ELECTRIC/COSY – Herrings Lane

1913-1957   Demolished

The foundation stone, laid by Elijah Southerland, recorded this building as a public hall, but it soon became the Electric Cinema, later renamed the Picture House.

Its nearness to many scattered villages in North Norfolk brought it success as a popular rural cinema. People travelled in by cycle or pony cart and a bus service run by George Hubbard.

The balcony afforded the best view with its plush seats but heavy rain caused terrible noise on the corrugated roof.

During the 1920s the proprietor was J. Loveday, while Herbert Wells, a travelling cinema showman from Hunstanton, who earned the title "Bert the Picture Man", took the lease in 1933.

Eventually it was acquired by East Coast Cinemas Ltd., in collaboration with the Bostock circuit and was renamed The Cosy from 1936. For much of this later time it was managed from the Wells Regal.

CROMER

REGAL – Hans Place

1914-Open

This cinema, almost a next door neighbour of the church, opened as Cromer Theatre of Varieties presenting films, live shows and boxing, on August 14th, 1914. It was created by the partnership of Edward Troller; a fruit shop owner along with a local butcher and farmer. Within two months it became a popular retreat for soldiers billeted in the town as England entered the First World War.

Talking pictures were installed by Victor Harrison who rented the theatre and reopened in 1930 with "Love Parade" starring Maurice Chevalier and Jeanette MacDonald. The following year, Victor Harrison renamed it The Central from Christmas Day. It was later extensively modernised, enlarged and redecorated so much that the old shell was unrecognisable. At this stage it became known as The Regal *"Norfolk's new super cinema"* reopening on 30th April, 1936 with the Fred Astaire and Ginger Rogers film "Top Hat".

The Regal became a valuable asset for the resort of Cromer, often opening before its official performance times, when the weather was wet, to provide a welcome retreat for holiday-makers. But after 40 years service it closed at the end of the 1976 summer season – a victim of falling audiences.

The cinema stood vacant and decaying while on the property market for £27,000. It was eventually leased to North Norfolk District Council and there were numerous suggestions for the building's future which did not achieve fruition.

In 1977 the Regal was sub-let to local property developer, Frank Boswall, who managed to reopen the cinema with good intent on 25th September. Four years later a further leasing brought it under the control of Ace Cinemas Ltd, but alas, their compulsory liquidation forced another closure in January, 1985.

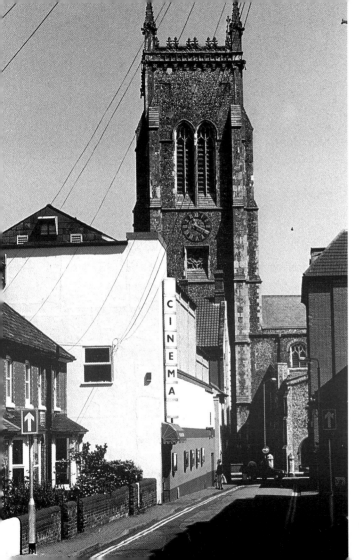

In April 1985 The Regal was 'saved' with enthusiasm by film producer Simon Perry and Alistair Gregory of Film Network UK who reopened with "A Passage to India". Through circumstance, Simon Perry had realised a boyhood dream of owning a cinema and what better hands to control the Regal. He was in the forefront of Britain's revived film industry, producing successful films such as "1984" and "Another Time, Another Place".

The new owners embarked on a £140,000 face-lift supported by a local council grant which regenerated the cinema in a 1930s style. Unfortunately the public support never reached all expectations, which resulted in the forming of the Norfolk Cinema Trust in January 1988 with the aim of securing the Regal's future.

In a surprise deal later that year the Regal was sold to David High and Chris Green, film enthusiasts who had also realised a dream of running their own cinema. They implemented improvements throughout and modified the Regal to four screens by July 1994.

Despite its few periods of closure, the Regal remains the oldest cinema operating in the county.

CROMER

OLYMPIA – Garden Street

1934-1939 Demolished

Norman Troller, pictured outside The Olympia in 1974, is the son of the man who built the Regal in Hans Place.

The Olympia started life as an open air Theatre with deck chairs and a stage on the lawn of London House in Garden Street. Eventually it was roofed over and became a Theatre for live shows, listed as the Olympian Gardens, in 1931.

Victor Harrison, the local cinema entrepreneur, leased the building as a cinema in 1934 for summer seasons. There were shows twice nightly; matinees Monday and Thursday and other days "if wet".

After use as a cinema it became a rifle range before being converted to a skating rink and music venue by Norman Troller for the years 1947-1974.

DEREHAM (EAST)

CINEMA – 64 Norwich Street

1915-1939 Change of Use

This is the facade of the town's memorial Hall, a centre for entertainments and functions. It was Elvin's Coach Works before becoming The Dereham and District Picture Palace. In the 1930s it doubled as a swimming pool with the water boarded-over during the winter months to serve as a cinema auditorium. It was named The Mayfair during the 1940s and managed in conjunction with the Exchange Cinema in the Market Place.

Both cinemas shared the newsreel for many years. When the film had been shown here an operator would take it to the Exchange, wait while it was screened and then return it to Norwich Street for the next showing.

Cinema shows ceased after the last war but returned in 1973 for two years when Colin Aldis set-up for the period while his CBA Exchange was turned over to bingo.

The building was refurbished as the town's memorial to the fallen of World War Two.

DEREHAM (EAST)

HOLLYWOOD (FORMERLY EXCHANGE/CBA) – Market Place

1926-Open

East Dereham's Corn Exchange, built in 1857, with its impressive front of Corinthian Columns became the town's silent cinema with one floor and a screen painted on the back wall. The building was heavily modified for "talking pictures" when a circle was added and a proscenium built forward of the old silent screen to serve the cinemas golden period of the 1930s up to the Second World War. Even a bomb shattering one side of its pitched roof during an enemy raid did not thwart its survival.

Dwindling audiences in the 1950s were countered by reducing the Exchange's capacity in 1961 to create a dance hall in the stalls area and cinema in the circle.

Much of its recent survival is owed to Colin Aldis who leased the Exchange from 1965-1992 and promoted his initials, CBA, as the cinema's name.

Colin had worked at the Exchange from the age of 14 and vowed that Dereham would always have a cinema while he was able to operate. There was a break in operation from May 1973 to 1976 when bingo took over and Colin temporarily took over the Memorial Hall. As leases and ownerships of the building changed in recent years the future of the cinema was periodically under threat.

With the need to survive the competitive world of film supply, the CBA was taken on by Trevor Wicks, the regions newest entrepreneur. He reopened in 1992 under the new name of Hollywood and is maintaining the cinema in Dereham, with the help of Colin and Miriam Aldis, running in conjunction with operations at Great Yarmouth and Lowestoft.

DISS

PICTURE HOUSE – Victoria Road

1916-1973 Vacant

Sullings and Company were the proprietors of the first cinema here in 1916 on a site occupied by the car park of the present building. It was destroyed by fire and rebuilt as the New Picture House in 1934 by Mr. E. Stevens whose other interest was a threshing business. During the second war live shows were presented when a stage was set up in front of the screen.

Jack Jones moved from Wales to be the first manager and became the owner in 1964. His enthusiasm kept the business going as long as possible, until March 1973, when the cinema closed one Saturday evening with just forty patrons for the final performance. Norwich City's League Cup Final at Wembley had drawn the rest of the usual Saturday night patrons.

The decline was also burdened by the constant cost of repairs caused by vandalism of the seating by young people.

Soon after closure a proposal was put forward that the local council should buy the cinema for community use but it never reached fruition. After some time the building was taken over as commercial premises for many years before becoming vacant once more.

DOWNHAM MARKET

ELECTRIC – Paradise Road

1913-1932 Demolished

London and Eastern Counties Cinemas Ltd built and equipped this classic example of the period. It became affectionately known as 'Chadwicks' through being managed by Mr & Mrs Francis Chadwick.

Mrs Chadwick would sell tickets at the kiosk while her husband was inside tearing them in two as patrons entered, before dashing upstairs to attend the film projector. Sometimes, he managed to perform all three jobs. Francis was also the local photographer who was based in Paradise Road and is credited as having taken this picture of the cinema.

The exterior of the Electric was illuminated at night by gas-burning lamps which hissed and spluttered in rainy weather. The gas for the engine which powered the generator to make electricity for the film projector was supplied from a bag at constant pressure. As the gas was used and the pressure became low it would be increased by employing the services of a heavy boy who would sit on the bag.

The Electric did not survive the coming of 'talking pictures' and closed when a modern cinema, the Regent, was opened in 1932. Mr Chadwick was engaged to work at the new cinema but soon realised he was unqualified to deal with the operation so he retired.

Paradise Road, Downham

Chadwick

DOWNHAM MARKET

REGENT – High Street

1932-1976 Change of use

Provincial Amusements Ltd built this modern cinema with a capital of £10,000 on the site of the old Post Office. Its construction required so much excavation that an alternative site was considered but the extra cost was prohibitive.

It opened in 1932 with "The Sport of Kings" a Gainsborough film of 1931; the story of a strict JP who inherits a bookmaking business.

While construction was in progress, when the scaffolding was still in place on the facade, a Downham Market boy, John Browne, came home from his London school and was smitten by the sight of the new Regent. His local friends were agog when he spoke of the 'talking pictures' he had seen in London and he knew the path of his career was with the cinema. He eventually took work at the Regent as apprentice projectionist in 1936 until leaving for war service. On return he became chief operator and then manager.

John Browne's greatest accomplishment in almost 40 years at the cinema was taking Twentieth Century Fox to task, single handed, over a wrangle preventing him showing "The Sound of Music" in 1966. He strode into their London office and made clear his demands which resulted in the Regent getting the film and earned him applaud from the distributor.

In the declining stages of the Regent's time John Browne booked "The Sound of Music" once again for the final show on Saturday, 2nd October, 1976 to make it an occasion to remember. This time Twentieth Century Fox had to make a copy available from America.

After sale by auction in 1977, the Regent became a Cycle Museum, a wood turnery centre and latterly an antique furniture shop.

FAKENHAM

CENTRAL – Market Place

1931-1976 Change of use

Fakenham Cinema Ltd created the Central in the shell of the 1855 Corn Hall. It had once been the Magistrates Court and a library of 6,000 volumes. Talking pictures in Fakenham were first seen and heard at the Central and from 1950 it was owned by Eastern Theatres Ltd., run in conjunction with the Regent at Downham Market.

In the early days, operation costs were kept to a minimum with very little outlay. The Central had been equipped with second-hand projection machinery, most of which was not replaced until the 1950s. This was often the attitude of the early operators.

Originally a diesel engine was used to generate electricity and it is reputed that when a projector's arc-lamp was 'struck' all the coloured lights around the top of the building would go out.

Much of the Central's later survival was due to the manager, George Mayes, who lived 'over the shop'. He had booked films for the cinema since 1965 and knew the people of his district. But continuing success was dependent on the films being available. Typically, a popular film of 1974 was "Enter the Dragon", advertised on television as being shown 'everywhere' but what the distributors meant was 'everywhere a copy is available' and that may not have been Fakenham.

Dwindling audiences during the hot summer months, high rates and increased film transport costs all contributed to the forced closure in October 1976. Norman Jacobs from Wisbech took over and staged bingo which continues at the present with the current operator.

FAKENHAM

ELECTRIC PAVILION/REGAL – Holt Road

1920-1940 Change of use

This former Territorials Drill Hall, built at the time of the South African War, became a skating rink before conversion to a cinema in 1920, with 'talking pictures' first shown in 1931. It was renamed the Cinema Pavilion Theatre in 1937, then Regal in May of that year in time for the film of King George VI's Coronation.

CINEMA – Norwich Road

1916-1931 Change of use

This ancient entrance dating from 1886 was part of the British School for boys, girls and infants of Fakenham. The town's early 'silent' cinema opened here and it was run by Mr H.E. Howell of the Fakenham Cinema Company with George Baxter as manager in 1916 who was "crazy on cinemas". It closed in 1931 when the Central opened in the Market Place and was turned into a bazaar selling all kinds of goods.

20

FELTWELL

Rex – High Street

1940-1959 Vacant

The 450 seat Coronation Hall of 1911 was the venue for early travelling film shows. It was converted to a cinema to attract patrons from Feltwell's RAF station but there was competition from the base's own cinema.

Ben Culey of the Palace, Thetford ran it for some years to spread the bookings with his other cinemas. In March 1988 it was converted to a snooker hall but is now closed.

GORLESTON

Pavilion – Pavilion Road

1908-1919 Open as a Variety Theatre

The Pavilion was a public hall of 1901 with film shows and variety staged by George Gilbert of Gt. Yarmouth's Hippodrome who ran it as The Palace. It was taken over by F.H. Cooper for a season of films in 1919.

GORLESTON

FILMLAND – Beach Road

1913-1930 Demolished

The name was ahead of its time but this was changed on a few occasions. Pictured here as the Palace it was also called The Playhouse, Scala and Louise Quatorze. The last name was aborted by locals to become 'Lousy Quarters'.

Filmland was Gorleston's first real cinema; a collaboration of F.H. Cooper and local auctioneer A.V. George. It was designed by local architect G. Reeve and built by B.G. Beech of Great Yarmouth.

It opened 21st July, 1913, with "1812" a production of Napoleon's retreat from Moscow with piano accompaniment by Mr Bert Hutchings.

Pathe Gazette provided the principal news of the world in living pictures.

The opening of Filmland provided an important incursion into the business for Douglas Attree, who arrived in Gorleston to take the post of operator and electrician, later progressing to open his own cinema.

GORLESTON

Palace – High Street

1939-1964 Change of use

The last cinema to open in Norfolk before World War II. The Palace, with 1000 seats, designed by architect Norman Bailey for a London Company, Rickenya Ltd, occupied the site of Gorleston's old Post Office.

Boxing Day 1938 had been the projected opening date but building work was delayed by a crisis holding up supplies of steel. It opened on January 16th, 1939 with "Snow White and the Seven Dwarfs".

The new cinema was in competition with the Coliseum, in the High Street since 1914, but at the opening ceremony the Mayoress emphasised that Gorleston could support two cinemas. After the war the Palace was bought by Raymond Stross Cinemas then sold in 1957 to Clifford Spain, Stross' Circuit Manager.

The structure has been 'saved' through the operation of bingo.

GORLESTON

COLISEUM – 141 High Street

Aug 1913-Jan 1970 Demolished

The Coliseum with its wide classical front incorporating shops either side of the entrance opened on August Bank Holiday, 1913 with "The Mysteries of Paris".

At the time of this photograph it was showing "The Road to Mandalay", a silent film of 1926 starring Lon Chaney.

Ernest Valentine Barr, a local cinema impresario promoted the Coliseum in partnership with Douglas Attree, an electrical engineer from Kings Lynn power station, who had arrived in Gorleston to 'wire' Filmland in Beach Road. This began a life-long association with the cinema for the Attree family with Douglas Attree jnr managing the Coliseum after the death of his father in 1945.

The architecture of the cinema was drastically altered in 1937 to bring it in line with the new theatres which had been appearing since the advent of 'talking pictures'. A false front was added incorporating a vertical fin carrying the name in modern lettering. Douglas Attree jnr maintained the Coliseum as the resort's most popular cinema for over 40 years and managed to outlive the modern Palace just a short distance away. He knew his patrons, could strike good bargains with film distributors and dealt with unsavoury elements in that period when cinemas became trouble spots sparked by younger patrons.

The Coliseum staved of all opposition except the plight of dwindling audiences and closed in January 1970 showing "Monte Carlo or Bust".

GREAT YARMOUTH

THE GEM/WINDMILL – Marine Parade

1908- Change of use

This developed into Norfolk's first permanent cinema when it should have been a show place for wild animals. Local opposition forced the change of scheme by C.B. Cochran (later famous impresario) who launched this continuous cinema show as 'Electric Vaudeville'. He upset the Gt. Yarmouth authorities so much that they imposed a restriction on the Gem's licence, insisting that men and women could not sit together in the dark! Each were confined to their own side of the auditorium.

Ben Jay and son Jack from London acquired it in 1938 and it was requisitioned for the Second World War. The Jays renamed it the Windmill in 1945 and staged highly successful runs of variety. Jack kept his cinematograph licence renewed "just in case" and Jack's son Peter maintained the tradition with periodic cinema.

It is a listed historical building and now houses "Ripley's Believe it or Not" exhibition.

GREAT YARMOUTH

Eᴍᴘɪʀᴇ – Marine Parade

1911-1991 Change of use

This was Gt. Yarmouth's first building designed purely for films and remains a fine example of its period; secure through a historical listing.

Opening on July 2nd, 1911 it was considered "an ornament to the Parade", with its front of Burmantoft's Vitreous Terra-cotta in the free Renaissance Style. Some of the decorative stonework was removed when its decay brought fear of it falling.

The Empire was another venture by Ernest Valentine Barr a local impresario.

It was acquired by the Jays in 1938 and run by them for many years as the Empire Picture Playhouse. Bingo sustained the business for many seasons but cinema returned full time in 1985. Towards the end of its time the battle between bingo and cinema was constant.

In August 1996 it re-opened as a "Theme Street" featuring eight bars and a Hollywood Cafe inspired by the cinema.

27

GREAT YARMOUTH

REGENT – Regent Road

1914-1982 Change of use

The Regent was a most ambitious project for East Anglia's own 'cinema magnate' F.H. Cooper (he became president of the Cinema Exhibitors Association in 1929). The design of this most beautiful cinema was the work of Wisbech Architect Francis Burdett Ward. Equipped for films and stage shows, with an auditorium decorated in the rich styles of Louis XLV it was likened to the London Coliseum when it opened on Boxing Day 1914.

Building progress had been hindered by one occupant of a property on the site. Unlike his neighbours he had refused to sell so the shell of the theatre continued to be built around his cottage until he was forced to move.

The Regent accommodated 1,679 patrons fifty of whom could pay for the privilege of a box. They could walk on 2,000 yards of best Wilton carpet, gaze upon Lister velvet curtain and draperies, the like of which they may never see in their homes. *(The photograph on page 30 shows the original interior in all its splendour).*

The cinema's colossal frontage was its main advertisement in 1914 and some of it remains to this day. The wrought-iron canopy over the pavement has gone but the fine stone-carved panels representing music, literature and art, with the masks of comedy and tragedy, continue to gaze down.

The Regent presented many years of cine-variety before turning purely to films. It was eventually acquired by the ABC circuit and survived as a cinema until September 25th, 1982.

With its future undecided, a vociferous campaign to project the fabric of this unique building was rewarded by a Department of Environment Grade 2 listing in October 1982. Bingo is the saviour of its relatively intact structure.

GREAT YARMOUTH

CENTRAL/PLAZA – Market Place

1915-1939 Demolished

This classic example of the period boasted a front of white stonework and seated 650 patrons. It opened Easter Monday 1915 with an exclusive film, 'Florence Nightingale', released in the preceding month.

In 1982 a change of ownership brought a new name, The Plaza. Victor Harrison (VEH cinemas) an established cinema entrepreneur leased it at a time when he thought he could do no wrong but lost money in its operation.

During the last war it became a temporary Marks & Spencers store when their town branch was bombed. It was vacant at the time of the 1953 floods so was used to store damaged furniture from the water ravaged homes of Palmers customers. Demolition came in 1958 to make way for Woolworths store.

31

GREAT YARMOUTH

Royal Aquarium/Royalty/Hollywood – Marine Parade

1914- Open

This vast building of 1883 was an aquarium which became a 2000 seat theatre in 1896 and played host to such illustrious names of the day as Lily Langtry and Ellen Terry with Ernest Shackleton and Oscar Wilde lecturing there.

Cinema shows were billed in 1914 under its lessee and later owner John Nightingale. He engaged stars of melodramas and musical comedy through the 1920s.

Full time cinema was presented for the introduction of the 'talkies' in 1931 with live shows staged during the summer months. Variety seasons were prominent from 1954 to 1967 when the neighbouring Britannia Pier theatre had been destroyed by fire. The Royal Aquarium then reverted to films until acquisition by the Forte Group. The new owners spent £80,00 in face-lifting the building and created a second cinema out of the adjoining repertory theatre. The revamped main cinema, seating 1,100 and boasting a 50ft wide screen, the biggest in East Anglia, opened on May 14th, 1970.

The name change to Royalty came with its acquisition by Peter Jay in 1982 and so began another ten year period of films and variety.

In a change of fortunes the complex was taken over in January 1992 by Trevor Wicks, a young man with the entrepreneurial spirit which has been present all through cinema history. In 1996 he added two more auditoriums in the main hall and renamed the four screen centre "Hollywood" along with his other cinemas at East Dereham and Lowestoft.

GREAT YARMOUTH
REGAL – Regent Road

1934-1988 Demolished

The Regal opened as a "£50,000 monument to local enterprise", the realisation of a dream long cherished by a group of Great Yarmouth's businessmen. It was built on the site of the former Theatre Royal from the designs of corroborating architects, Yates, Cook & Derbyshire of London and Olly & Hayward of Gt. Yarmouth. The construction went through turbulent times with two builders getting into 'money difficulties' and the work was taken up to completion by John Balls & Son *(the workmen engaged on the Regal are shown on page 36)*.

The design requirements had created one of the steepest of rakes seen in any balcony *(page 37)* and throughout its life usherettes were never happy being on duty there.

The grand opening on January 21st, 1934 was more exciting than many of the new cinemas of that period because a film star, Merle Oberon, was present at the opening ceremony. She played the part of Anne Boleyn in the Regal's first film "The Private Life of Henry VIII".

Reginald New, a popular broadcasting organist of the time played the National Anthem to open the proceedings on the Compton organ as it rose from the orchestra pit. The Mayor, Councillor Percy Ellis performed the opening accompanied on stage by Mr. Ernest Barr the Regal's Managing Director. The assembled audience was told how the film to be shown had been made for £10,000 more than it had cost to build the new cinema.

The Regal served its 54 years with cinema and variety shows in the summer months with various takeovers and acquisitions until the retreating public prevented its survival.

GREAT YARMOUTH
HIPPODROME – St. Georges Road
1903-1940 Open as a circus

Built for circus variety by George Gilbert in 1903 The Hippodrome included 'moving pictures' in its bill of fare from the start. A screen would be fixed across the 42ft diameter circus ring, halfway between the expensive and cheaper seats.

In July 1908 the Hippodrome presented the Biblical epic film "The Sign of the Cross". Years later during the autumn and winter months a proscenium with stage and screen was erected on the west side of the auditorium allowing it to operate as a theatre and cinema with stage shows proceeded by 'short films' in the winter months. Circus shows were staged during the summer season, an alternating practice which continued into the 1940s.

It remains one of the country's oldest cinema venues.

HARLESTON

PICTURE HOUSE – Market Place

1920-1962 Change of use

Halfway along Exchange Street, is the entrance of what was once the smallest cinema in England. The original foyer leads through to the former auditorium (which seated just 178 patrons), and a raised area which once supported the projection-room. All are now part of a furniture shop.

Memories abound of double seats for courting couples and the assistant projectionist, Ernie Thurston, who was a maltster by day. Mrs Kenyon accompanied the silent films and moved to the paybox to sell tickets after 'talking pictures' were installed.

Mrs Bates, the proprietress, who owned the cinema for most of its later time is seen here on the right of the photograph. The occasion was a promotional stunt in the foyer.

When Cinemascope, the widescreen invention of 1954, was installed at a great expense, the Picture House proudly advertised the system over the front entrance for the rest of its days.

HOLT

THE CINEMA – High Street

1916-1940 Demolished

The tiny entrance dwarfed by Holt's war memorial led to the town's first cinema. With 450 seats it was situated behind the buildings on the plain in premises of the Norwich Co-operative Society. D.J. Larner was the proprietor.

The Electric Cinema is remembered for its corrugated iron roof which could leak in wet weather.

In March 1937 there was a fire in the cinema at the time of screening of the film "Lone Wolf Returns".

Bert Wells, a touring exhibitor from Hunstanton, also presented talking pictures in Holt at this time, at the Co-Op Hall in New Street.

The High Street cinema closed soon after the modern Regal was opened in Peacock Lane.

HOLT

REGAL – Peacock Lane

1937-1962 Change of use

This 'super' was built as part of a small chain by East Coast Cinemas Ltd and opened 8th March, 1937 with the film "Texas Rangers". Eventually it was taken into the Bostock Cinema Circuit and was one of the first cinemas in the county to be allowed to open on Sundays under the Regulation 42B. This wartime legislation allowed the cinema to provide entertainment for servicemen and as a result there were visits from Jimmy Handley and Richard Murdoch, two radio personalities, stationed locally.

After the war, the seven day operation continued, provided Sunday opening did not clash with Church service times.

Baron Pert, the long serving manager enjoyed the best business ever in the years 1940 to 1946 but in the decline by the early 1960s the closure was swift. He walked into the bank one morning and was given the closing date by the manager. The Regal re-opened as a bingo hall, then became a snooker hall.

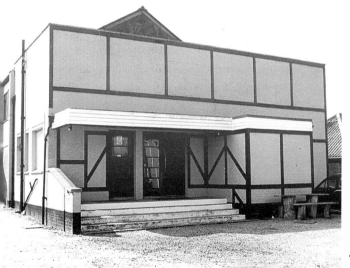

HUNSTANTON

CAPITOL/PRINCESS THEATRE – The Green

1932- Open

This impressive theatre was built as a joint venture by Ben Culey and Ernie Adams, two King's Lynn businessmen who had faith in cinema. The 700 seat Capitol, equipped for live shows, was designed by King's Lynn architect Keeble Allflat and built in Norfolk carstone, a material quarried at Snettisham. The theatre is unique for having the largest gable ever constructed in the local stone.

Charles Le Strange of Hunstanton Hall opened the Capitol on 22nd June, 1932 when the 'big film' was "The Desert Song" starring John Boles and Carlotta King.

The proprietors were justly proud of their new theatre when stating "we have given you the best, give us your support". They staged films and good plays and soon after opening brought "The Barretts of Wimpole Street" from the Queen's Theatre, London for three nights.

The cinema survived until closure in 1960 then reopened for a time as the Capitol Bingo Club. A new owner, Peter Smith, subsequently took over and renamed it The Kingsley Centre in 1969 putting on Gilbert & Sullivan and some films. The most significant change came when the local council bought the theatre in 1981 and renamed it The Princess in honour of locally-born Lady Diana Spencer.

For a while the theatre was managed by the late Dick Condon of Norwich's Theatre Royal. The old projection equipment was removed but films returned for a season by an installation of temporary equipment. Subsequent complete refurbishing and re-equipping for film presentation has produced a successful theatre putting on a variety of entertainment of which the local management can be proud.

HUNSTANTON

MIKADO – Seafront

1920-1924 Demolished

Early cinema shows were presented by an Italian showman in the Mikado Concert Hall, a 200 seat wooden pavilion.

Louis Herbert Wells of Northcote House, Hunstanton, who became affectionately known as "Bert the Picture Man", leased the hall for a season in 1923 but the cinema was destroyed by fire the following year.

TOWN HALL – The Green

1896- Change of use

Before the Capitol was opened on The Green, Herbert Wells operated regular cinema shows in the Town Hall as did Raymond Rayner another of the county's cinema entrepreneurs.

The Town Hall of 1896 was the resort's main theatrical venue for many years. It was refurbished for general community use and the Tourist Information Centre in 1994.

44

KING'S LYNN

ELECTRIC THEATRE – Broad Street

1911-1938 Demolished

This cinema brought F.H. Cooper to Norfolk. He was a young estate agent from Wisbech who had become smitten with the medium of 'moving pictures' after going to a fairground cinema show. He opened the Electric on 23rd September, 1911 with the slogan "The Most Comfortable Hall in the District". The cinema's last pianist for the silent films, Dorothy MacDonald, once recalled, *"Sometimes I had a sheet telling me what music was required, otherwise I made it up myself. I played for a lot of serials keeping one eye on the music and the other on the screen"*.

The Electric survived a few years of the talkies and closed on April 9th, 1938 after showing "The Bad Guy". It saw use as an Army barracks in the last war and then became part of Taylors Garage before demolition in 1969 to make way for town development.

45

KING'S LYNN

EMPIRE – Broad Street

1913-1929 Demolished

This was the second venture by F.H. Cooper. He refurbished this old Free Christian Church which had been a make-shift cinema called the Albion Hall.

The narrow site of 70 x 27 ft sandwiched between the City of Norwich Pub and houses had restricted its expansion to a decent size cinema. Cooper gutted and refurbished the building and incorporated so many safety features that the insurance premium was reduced by 70% of that charged to the previous operators.

The Empire opened on the 30th April, 1913 under the management of George Starkey who later became a noted cinema manager in Norwich. The Empire was never 'wired for sound' and was demolished after being left in a decaying state for many years.

46

KING'S LYNN

ST JAMES THEATRE – County Court Road

1921-1937 Demolished

This theatre was the result of rebuilding after fire destroyed a public hall on the site. Films were shown there at the St James in 1914, it became a Picture Palace in 1921. It was the first King's Lynn cinema to show 'talking pictures' on September 2nd, 1929 with "The Singing Fool". A fire destroyed the theatre on 11th February, 1937.

THEATRE ROYAL – St James Street

1938-1960 Change of use

This was another fire-ravaged site with the current Theatre Royal replacing two burned predecessors. All had presented films; the present being the purest cinema, opened on 4th April, 1938 with "The Prisoner of Zenda". It operated with rear-projection until the arrival of Cinemascope in 1955 when a 30 foot curved screen was installed.

By 1960 it had closed as a cinema.

KING'S LYNN
MAJESTIC – Tower Street
1928- Open

This was the last Norfolk cinema to be built in the era of the silent film. It was the ultimate in design by architects H.L. Carnell and W.D. White who gave the building its impressive clock-tower roofed in copper. The complex of cinema, ballroom and café took eight months to complete.

Mr Ernest Adams, the Majestic's promoter, had purchased the whole of the interior of the Empire, Leicester Square, London including its fine mahogany panelling and mirrors which were renovated and installed in the ballroom.

The opening on 23rd May, 1928 was marked by the presentation of the epic film "Ben Hur" accompanied by special effects and music supplied by the orchestra with sacred hymns and pieces sung by the choir of South Lynn All Saints Church. With "Ben Hur", made in 1925, the art of the silent film was regarded in America as having reached its summit. In England, the new Majestic cinema was considered the last word in luxurious 'picture theatres'.

From the beginning the Majestic was upheld as a "super cinema" with seating for 1000 patrons and soon became labelled one of the finest in the Eastern Counties. But the grand launch was overshadowed by a few problems. The cinema's notable clock tower feature was waiting for its copper dome and wrought-iron weather vane. It was a month or more before the cafe opened and the ballroom would not be completed until the dancing season began.

A year and two months later the beginning of the end for silent films at the Majestic came with the screening of its first 'talking picture', "The Perfect Alibi", in July 1929.

The ballroom with its sprung floor used to host the West Norfolk Hunt Ball each year and is often recalled for its unique supper dances going on into the early hours. In 1932 it hosted Oscar Logan and his Black and White Syncapators.

The successful operation of the Majestic made it a prime acquisition for Union Cinemas which later became ABC under whose banner it ran until company changes at national level put the cinema on the open market. It was acquired in 1975 by local joint owners Tony Rowlett and Malcolm Croot who set about creating the present Majestic Film Centre.

The ballroom was converted to a second auditorium in 1977 and four years later a third 'screen' was installed in the ground floor stalls area.

Cinemas like the Majestic survive because of the passion of their owners. In 1988, Tony Rowlett and Malcolm Croot along with the town's Lions Club organised a gala evening to celebrate the building's sixty years. It was a nostalgic revival for what remains a fitting monument to the era of the early cinema.

KING'S LYNN
PILOT – John Kennedy Road
1938-1983 Change of use

The tiled canopy is a recent addition to this ultimate in modern 'supers' launched by Ben Culey, a colourful local character, farmer and fishing smack owner. Keeble Allflat of King's Lynn was the architect and it took fourteen weeks to build. The cinema took its name from Pilot Street now renamed John Kennedy Road.

Its special design introduced a 'stadium' arrangement for the seating, one great sweep with no balcony, accommodating 797 patrons with some double seats for courting couples. There were dressing rooms and a stage for live shows.

The Pilot opened 28th November with the memorable Walt Disney production of "Snow White and the Seven Dwarfs", a unique occasion because no other cinema in the district had managed to book this famous film. The patrons on that first night were mostly the friends and associates of Ben Culey.

It also played a part in film production when the King's Lynn area was used for location scenes for the 1943 production "The Silver Fleet" starring Ralph Richardson. The film from each days shoot, the 'rushes', were screened at The Pilot to check their quality.

The cinema closed in 1961 but was reopened a year later by the partnership of Tony Rowlett and Malcolm Croot. A second and final closure came on 27th March, 1983 with the epic film "Ghandi". It was sold for conversion to a snooker hall, joined by a hardware and builders merchants and later a skating rink. It is now vacant.

9260   NORWICH ROAD. MATTISHALL

MATTISHALL

ELECTRIC – Dereham Road & Burgh Lane

1916-1927 Demolished

This picture portrays a time when life was moving at a very gentle pace and the cinema had found its place in the most rural of communities.

The wooden building on the left was the Oddfellows Hall of 1916 which was taken two days each week for the visiting show of Gordon Arthur Fickling from Ovington. He was a farmer's son who had been drawn like so many others by the magic of moving pictures. In one of his advance publicity announcements he proclaimed: *"You now have the opportunity of seeing one of the World's Masterpieces in Motion Pictures, which will be shown at the Electric Cinema, Mattishall for One night Only, Friday, September 30th "Damaged Goods" (Adults only). This great production has broken all records wherever shown. Remember! You may never have this opportunity of seeing such a Grand Picture. The film has been shown at Watton and Shipdham, by Special Request"*.

This 1914 silent version of a story, rightfully billed for adults only, which had an awful warning, concerned a young man who infects his wife and child with syphilis.

NORTH WALSHAM

REGAL – New Road

1931-1977 Change of use

This was the first 'picture house' in Norfolk to be designed and built specifically for 'talking pictures', by the regions newest cinema entrepreneur, Victor Harrison. J. Owen Bond, also new to the business, was the architect who designed the 585 seat cinema on modern principles. The interior decor was the work of Norwich decorative plasterers, Crotch & Sons who introduced an Egyptian style with a ceiling in motifs of terra cotta lotus flowers in orange, blue and green.

Thomas Gill and Sons built the Regal for £3,000. They had been quick to tender for the work in the depressed times of the building industry. This was their first cinema and only just ahead of Norwich's new Carlton, which had also been priced for Victor Harrison, but North Walsham's Regal was taken up first.

The opening ceremony on 7th September, 1934 was performed by Guy Fanshawe, East Norfolk's prospective Conservative Candidate and the 'big film' that night was "A Warm Corner" starring Leslie Hanson.

In its later years the Regal played a dual role along with bingo sessions.

After closure it stood vacant before conversion to motor vehicle dealerships and is currently an industrial tool-hire depot.

NORTH WALSHAM

PICTUREDROME – Kings Arms Street

1912-1931 Change of use

This conversion of an earlier premises was taken on by John Dixon, a lively man of the town. The plain small building offered a cosy retreat despite its lack of refinery. There was one floor, raked at the rear and a box with six chairs for special patrons.

Harold and Lydia Coates came from London to manage the place for all its life. They ran the shows with very little help; Mr Coates produced publicity material and maintained the generator as there was no mains supply then. Kings Arms Street would be a blaze of light from the illumination on the facade.

Harld Coates, *(Right in photograph)* operated the projector when his assistant *(left)* was called to serve in the First World War.

The Picturedrome survived only a week after the new Regal opened in New Road. After closure it had various uses and is now a carpet showroom.

56

NORWICH

ELECTRIC THEATRE – 102-104 Prince of Wales Road

1912-1961 Demolished

This cinema established F.H. Cooper in Norwich, the estate agent from Wisbech, who had been captivated by 'moving pictures' at the turn of the century. The ornate 'picture theatre' designed by his architect friend and business neighbour in Wisbech, Francis Burdett Ward, was the forerunner of many cinema designs.

Variety turns and films were the combined fare with a fine resident orchestra accompanying the silent 'pictures'. There were regular promotions to advertise special films and when D.W. Griffith's masterpiece "Broken Blossoms" was released in 1920, starring Lilian Gish and Donald Crisp, the Electric's staff and some extras masqueraded as Chinese characters to portray a scene from the film. *(pictured on page 60)*

Talkies came in April 1929 with a five week run of "Sunny Side Up" when 89,000 people saw the film.

The Electric Theatre flourished for another twenty years but falling attendances and the need to upgrade the building brought change of ownership when it was taken by Victor Harrison. He revitalised its Edwardian styling to lose the Electric image and reopened as The Norvic on September 9th, 1949. *(see page 61)*

Harrison, being an independent exhibitor of some note was able to introduce the new widescreen system of Cinemascope to the Norvic on December 27th, 1954 with "The Robe", before his bigger competitors in the city.

Towards the end of its life, as audiences dwindled, there was an attempt to change course with foreign films but all to no avail. The last film was "Wild in the Country".

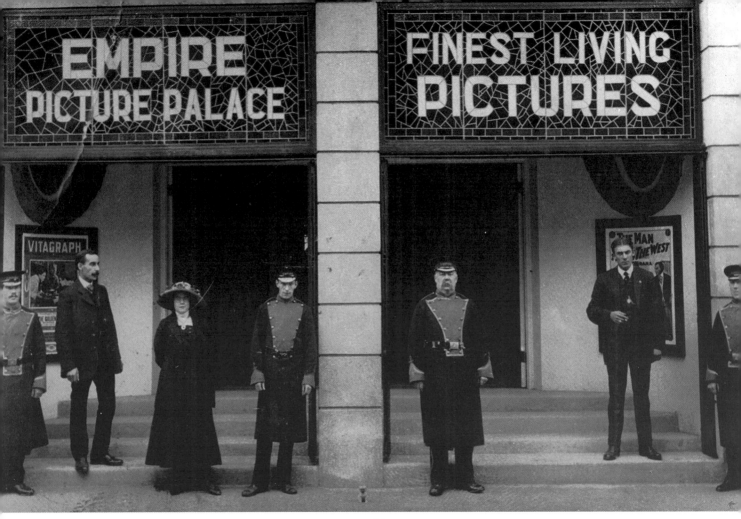

NORWICH

EMPIRE – 79 Oak Street

1913-1940 Demolished

This rare picture of the Empire's staff with commissionaires proudly displaying their military style uniforms records more tragedy than the stories shown on its flickering screen. The young man fourth from the left was Archiebald Page a commissionaire with his intended wife by his side. After their marriage he went off to France and was wounded and died in 1916 leaving his wife with their baby daughter. At the age of 22 Mrs Page died during the 1918 influenza epidemic but the child survived, cared for by her grandmother.

The Empire, neighbouring the church and mission hall served a highly populated community of narrow busy streets with shops and pubs. In recent years it has been recalled as a classic example of the cinemas worst reputation of a 'flea-pit' – in retrospect an unkind label. More affectionate recollections are of children gaining admission by presenting a jam-jar or rabbit skin at the paybox. It was an admirable gesture by the proprietor as the children were often poor. At least the Empire brought escape from their hum drum lives in what to them was absolute luxury.

The cinema saw the successful transition to sound films on 12th January, 1931 with "Sunny Side Up". The Empire continued for just nine years and after closing was destroyed during an air raid in April 1942.

NORWICH

PRINCE OF WALES – 110a Prince of Wales Rd.

1912-1922 Demolished

A 900 seat cinema created in the former New Assembly Rooms, opened in June 1912 with films and variety. Its creaking wicker chairs are recalled. This was another of F.H. Cooper's ventures and for a time he based his head office here.

The building finished its days as a popular 1950s dance hall, The Grosvenor Rooms. Grosvenor House now occupies the site.

THEATRE ROYAL – Theatre Street

1956-1985 Open

The present refurbished theatre was leased to Essoldo in 1956 who ran it mainly as a cinema and was the first in Norwich to present stereophonic sound with "South Pacific" in 1959. Later under ownership of Norwich City Council it operated as a cinema in the summer months. Its history has been marked with uncertainty as a venue for live theatre but is now operating successfully.

NORWICH
HIPPODROME – St. Giles Street

1903-1960 Demolished

Built as the Grand Opera House in 1903, it was renamed Hippodrome in 1904 and the variety acts were often concluded with a performance of 'The Hippodrome Bioscope' an early description of the film medium.

The theatre became a permanent cinema for 1930-1937 and in November 1934, as shown here, was screening a German made film 'Morgenrot'. The subject was Naval Warfare of 1914-18 – "a picture to abolish war". The film had been banned in Germany by Hitler and not allowed to be shown for a time in this country. The Hippodrome's management was praised for securing the film soon after the English ban was lifted.

Live shows returned to the theatre after its cinema period with further attempts at film presentations before sudden closure.

65

NORWICH

REGAL – 5-7 Dereham Road

1938-1958 Vacant

Norwich Builders Thomas Gill & Son built V.E. Harrison's Regal in four and a half months. Seating 914 in circle and stalls, this was another design of J. Owen Bond and its fabric components had to be modified to fit between the neighbouring properties. A special feature of the auditorium decor were low-relief plaster panels on either side of the proscenium. These were enhanced by concealed lighting.

The Regal was opened on 16th April, 1938 with the film "Rose Marie" starring Nelson Eddy and Jeanette Macdonald.

During the last war it sustained considerable damage when its roof was blown off during the blitz of April 1942.

The cinema made headline news in 1957 when it screened "Rock Around the Clock" the film featuring the latest dance craze Rock'n'Roll and starring Bill Haley and the Comets. Exuberant fans rioted and danced in the aisles and were chased out into the streets to be dispersed by the police. The management had expected trouble, as the film was causing a sensation in London.

In the declining years the owners tried to attract more patrons by installing a panoramic screen to take a much larger picture, by altering lenses on the projection equipment but at the expense of losing the top and bottom of the picture.

At the height of the decline the closure was sudden and the Regal stood vacant for many years before reopening as the Mayfair Bingo Club which in turn ceased in 1990.

NORWICH

RITZ – Dereham Road/Marl Pit Lane

1938-1960 Change of use

This was the last cinema to be built for V.E. Harrison designed on the same patterns as the Regal. Costessey builders, Sissen & Bugdale worked to a 21 week schedule in time for its opening on 10th September, 1938 with "Sabu, Elephant Boy".

The interior photograph shows the creation of the 678 seat 'atmospheric' auditorium wrought in stencil-work by Clark & Fenn, a firm from Clapham who specialised in cinema decor of the 1930s.

The Ritz's scheme was to attract an audience from the vast expanding housing estate of the Larkman and catch cinemagoers travelling in from the west of the county.

It served the local population well until sudden closure after the last showing of "Please Turn Over" on the Saturday night of 10th July, 1960.

After standing vacant for some time it became a motor vehicle tyre depot in 1961.

NORWICH

THE CAPITOL – Mile Cross, Aylsham Road

1932-1960 Change of use

Victor Harrison's second venture in the city opened on Boxing Day, 1932, without formal ceremony with a showing of "Tarzan the Ape Man". During the interval the management announced that it intended to show all the best British films. The Capitol was promoted as "Norwich's new suburban cinema" being a mile or so from the city centre on one of the main roads in from the rural areas. Harrison's aim was to attract audiences who would normally travel into the city cinemas along with those from the neighbouring and steadily expanding housing estates in the Mile Cross area. There was the added advantage of car parking although there were few cars then.

The cinema's design had incorporated a circle but this was never constructed while the interior was described as being "attractively gay without being ornate".

After closure on 2nd April, 1960 the cinema was acquired and used to extend the Lido Ballroom next door to create The Norwood Rooms, a popular dance hall and function suite for many years. The whole dance hall complex closed to become the Mecca bingo centre.

NORWICH

CARLTON – All Saints Green

1932-1973 Change of use

The Carlton was the city's first cinema designed for the 'talkies' and another Victor Harrison project. Seating 900 patrons it was placed at a right-angle to the road and opened with "Politics" starring Marie Dressler in a programme which included live performances.

A year later the Carlton was acquired by Lou Morris who decided to extend the cinema to the size of the present building. *(the interior picture here shows the larger auditorium while the exterior appears on the front cover).*

The extended auditorium was built parallel to All Saints Green, on to the side of the original cinema with the new screen at the end of the addition, effectively turning it round. The wall between the two was removed in a feat of engineering which allowed the business to continue. At one point a glass screen was installed to allow films to be projected from the new projection box on to the new screen.

In 1939 the Carlton was taken in to the Odeon circuit and was changed in name to Gaumont when the old Gaumont closed in the Haymarket in 1959.

There were excursions into live shows and the installation of a vast projection system of 70mm films with six channels of sound during which time there were record runs of "The Sound of Music".

As the Gaumont, it survived well until closure in January 1973 to become the Top Rank bingo club.

NORWICH

CINEMA PALACE/MAYFAIR – 114-116 Magdalen Street

1912-1956 Demolished

This was Norwich's first purpose built cinema, as opposed to a reconstruction, the venture of Charles Thurston who had successfully introduced 'moving pictures' to the fairground crowds at the turn of the century. Norwich architects Morgan and Buckingham designed the Palace in the 'late English renaissance style'. The ornate exterior had been covered by a 'modern' tiled entrance when this photograph was taken at the time of the Festival of Britain in 1951.

The Cinema Palace was built entirely by local labour and a credit to all involved considering the work had been hampered by the 1912 floods in August. The flooding had affected the work on a unique feature of the cinema, a subway exit which led from the front of the auditorium to the street because the narrow site had not allowed for normal side exits.

Improved projection equipment and a special silver screen, the only one of its kind in Norwich, ensured the ultimate in film presentation.

The talkies came in December 1930 with an air drama called "Flight". The press reported that "The apparatus gave good results. The voices were audible and there was a complete absence of discordant noise".

The modern front was added in 1946 along with a new name, Mayfair. It was a popular cinema with its catchment area in the Magdalen Gates area of Norwich but was the first to close when the decline began after the last war.

The Mayfair closed in 1956 and fell into terrible decay before demolition for a bowling alley in the 1960s, which in turn failed. The structure is currently a studio for Anglia Television and the projected centre of its television news operation for East Anglia.

NORWICH
THE PICTURE HOUSE/GAUMONT
– Haymarket

1911-1959 Demolished

This was often claimed to be the city's premier cinema and began life as a small 372 seater constructed from the former London and Provincial Bank opening on 18th February, 1911. Soon after opening it proved inadequate in size but the war prevented development. It was almost completely demolished ten years later and rebuilt to seat 1700 patrons. In the photograph here *(and on page 79)* the original cinema's frontage can be seen on the right hand side of the building.

The reopening of the enlarged Picture House on 12th December 1921 by the Lord Mayor, H.M. Holmes, was an unprecedented occasion. The manager, Dan Benjamin, had invited two stars of the time, Mary Pickford and Douglas Fairbanks but they had to apologise by telegram for not attending. Then, uniquely, the new picture house was blessed by Canon Meyrick of St Peter Mancroft Church in whose parish the cinema was situated.

He hoped that religion, literature and art might flourish side by side and the audience stood for his blessing – "May thy spirit rest this day and forever on all who gather in this picture house".

The Picture House employed a gifted musical director, Sidney Skedge. He was deeply interested in arranging music for the silent films and was the city's highest paid musical director at £6 per week. Sidney would view a new film with the projectionist on Monday morning, enabling him to make notes of scene and mood changes.

Occasionally films came with a special score so the Monday morning run-through would be a chance to rehearse with the orchestra. *(picture on next page shows Sidney Skedge, standing, holding baton)*

Eight years later The Picture House was refurbished again, this time for the installation of talking pictures, the sixth cinema in England to be 'wired for sound'.

The stage was enlarged for variety turns but the main attraction was 'talking pictures' and the first to be presented was "The Singing Fool" with Al Jolson on 18th February, 1929. Contrary to popular belief, the orchestra at the Picture House was not thrown out of work overnight with the arrival of talking pictures. Several silent films had been in production and all would be presented as part of the programmes for some time.

In 1931 the Haymarket Picture House reverberated to the sound of the city's first cinema organ, a 3 manual Compton played by Leslie James. The instrument could provide every conceivable musical combination with a variety of sound effects for entertaining during the programme interludes. John Bee, a later organist, found fame in broadcasting on BBC radio and won the hearts of Norwich audiences.

Varied ownerships led to the cinema's acquisition by the Gaumont Picture Corporation, bringing a name change to Gaumont in 1955. But it was short lived and closed in 1959 when the name was transferred to the Carlton on All Saints Green.

After demolition, a Peter Robinson shop was built on the site which in turn became Top Shop.

NORWICH
REGENT/ABC/CANNON – Prince of Wales Road
1923- Open

This is the city's longest running cinema. It was built by The Alexandra Picture House and Theatre Co. who took its name from an existing 140ft frontage of shops, offices and accommodation called Alexandra Mansions. Part of this became the facade of the new 1800 seat theatre built behind the mansions and running from St. Faiths Lane. It was the most ambitious and the last successful project of F.H. Cooper and the last Norwich cinema in the 'silent' era.

It opened on 3rd December, 1923 with "The Prisoner of Zenda". It had taken 17 months to build from its stone laying ceremony on July 26th, 1922 an unusual occasion for cinemas.

From the beginning, The Regent was equipped for variety acts with a good stage, dressing rooms and orchestra pit. The elaborate ornate decor with much fibrous plasterwork adorned the auditorium. There were boxes either side of the stage and a fountain with goldfish pool in the foyer was a piece of living decor to behold for the arriving patrons. There was parking for cars in nearby Mountergate at "The Rink" and late arriving patrons unable to find seats could use the large "crush" room over the foyer and pass time reading periodicals provided.

After the talkies and acquisition by ABC much of the ornateness disappeared in 1961. The biggest change to the Regent was the tripling of its auditorium in 1973 under the EMI banner. A fourth smaller auditorium using a video format was created in the former restaurant. Further acquisitions brought the name Cannon and conversion of the fourth cinema to film.

'WONDER BAR'

THEATRE

CARLTON'S

NORWICH – REGENT/ABC (continued)

On the 29th October 1971 the cinema played host to a Royal Premiere when the Queen Mother attended a charity performance of "The Go Between", the film of L.P. Hartley's novel which had been filmed entirely on locations in Norfolk, mostly at Melton Constable.

In 1995 the cinema's ownership was changed again when much of its circuit was acquired by Richard Branson's Virgin organisation. Many of the cinemas in the chain, including this one, remained under a management buy-out resulting in a return to the name ABC Cinema. In the meantime there is one piece of the original architecture which remains out of reach but not out of sight in St Faiths Lane. Regent remains a firm etching of the theatre's illustrious days.

NORWICH

THATCHED THEATRE – All Saints Green

1915-1930 Demolished

By name alone this was a native of Norfolk and would have seemed to contravene the fire regulations, but apparently all conditions had been approved. It began life as the Thatched Assembly Rooms, comprising a restaurant and elegant ballroom and early in the first war had served as a billet for troops. The thatched front portion of the building housed the restaurant and provided the facade to the ballroom, which became the cinema auditorium on November 11th, 1915. The freehold belonged to the Bond family whose fashionable store was adjacent. The Thatched showed the best films accompanied by its fine string orchestra and served afternoon teas to attract an elite patronage. Providing the weather was fine a sliding roof would be opened to increase ventilation.

In March 1929, the Thatched screened "Shooting Stars" a love story set against the background of a film studio. Local people were attracted to it because a few scenes had been shot on Cromer beach and cliffs and it brought to prominence its young writer and assistant director Anthony Asquith, son of the Liberal Prime Minister.

The Thatched was never 'wired' for talkies and in August 1929 bravely advertised itself as "silent but sound". It survived with the silent films for a while until closure on April 12th, 1930. It reverted to use as a ballroom and became part of Bond's store until bombed during enemy action in the last war.

NORWICH

THEATRE DE LUXE – St Andrews Street

1910-1957 Demolished

This was the first building in Norwich designed for films, although its construction involved the conversion of former premises. It was also the first to bring the word 'cinema' to the public gaze and the first in Norwich to be established by a circuit.

The Theatre De Luxe was one of 14 'electric theatres' in London and eight in the provinces as far away as Plymouth and Southend owned by Electric Theatres 1908 Ltd. The reconstruction had incorporated part of a polytechnic institute dating from 1831 and formed an auditorium to seat 560 patrons. It opened to the public on 9th April, 1910 without ceremony and dignitaries, as people flowed in for the continuous performance from 2.30p.m. They paid 2d *(1p approx.)* admission for the stalls or 6d *(2.5p)* for the comfort of the balcony and saw "The Corsican's Revenge", "Generous Rivals" and "Dispensing with a Barber".

The new cinema's popularity proved that its capacity was inadequate so reconstruction brought an increase in size to seat 1000 patrons for a grand reopening September 28th, 1920.

The Theatre De Luxe was the last to convert to talking pictures in 1931 but the first to screen 3 Dimensional films in 1953 at a time when gimmicks were being introduced to stem the falling audiences. Through most of its latter days it was tagged 'The Ranch House' because of its seasons of Westerns.

NORWICH – THEATRE-DE-LUXE
(continued)

The decline in attendances coupled with its failure to meet safety standards brought sudden closure on 10th February, 1957. The film on the last night was "Outpost in Morocco", starring George Raft, made in 1949. The production had been labelled as too dull even for a children's matinee but the young people in the audience on the last night made it a memorable occasion. No doubt feeling cheated at losing their beloved venue they went berserk, tearing the place apart, damaging seats, ripping down the screen and reeling out the fire hoses. It was a sad climax for the manager, the late Archie Gibbs, a gifted musician who had joined the cinema business in the orchestra pit for the silent films. The building was allowed to fall into terrible decay before being demolished to provide a yard for the neighbouring telephone exchange.

NORWICH

ODEON – Botolph Street

1938-1971 Demolished

This was the city's only example of cinema 'brand marketing' started by a most remarkable businessman, Oscar Deutch. It was part of his sprawling chain which covered England in the 1930s and an operation which was likened to "a romance of finance". The Odeons were identifiable by their architectural similarities.

Norwich's Odeon with its 2054 seats was the biggest cinema north of London when it opened on 7th February, 1938. Its design was the work of Basil Herring, a notable cinema architect at that time and built by Stanley Leighton of Lowestoft. The vast frontage with the distinctive Odeon feature of faience tiling hid an enormous auditorium on a site cleared of several old buildings and courtyards.

The opening film was "The Sky's the Limit", a musical comedy. Lord Mayor, Charles Watling, performed the official ceremony and addressed the audience *"May this new Odeon begin a successful career of amusement, instruction and inspiration, that it will broaden men's minds, widen their vision and lift their souls above the cares of daily life"*.

The Odeon performed as Mayor Watling had wished until 1971 when it was demolished in favour of a replacement cinema which is part of the Anglia Square complex.

(Page 92 – the vast auditorium of the Odeon)

NORWICH

ODEON – Anglia Square

1971- Open

This replacement of the 1938 cinema was designed by Norwich architects Alan Cooke & Partners. The 1016 seater auditorium was on one sweeping level in the concept of a stadium. The interior decor for the concrete construction was provided by heavy drapes highlighted by subtle lighting.

A 48ft wide screen was served by Italian projection equipment, computerised to enable operation with a minimum of staff. The opening on July 8th, 1971 was performed by 'Miss Odeon', 19 year old Mary Flegg, chosen in a competition by readers of the Eastern Evening News. The first film was "Valdez is Coming" starring Burt Lancaster.

The new cinema won a major award for design later that year.

The continuously changing fortunes of the cinema business forced the owners, Rank Theatres Ltd to reconstruct the interior to provide three smaller auditoriums.

93

NORWICH

NOVERRE – Theatre Street

1950-1992 Change of use

The Noverre immortalised a Norwich family out of whose ballroom the 272 seat cinema was formed to screen films not always available on the commercial circuits. It is remembered with affection for no adverts, no ice cream, plenty of leg room and separate performances. It closed on December 23rd, 1992 after four years of falling ticket sales.

CINEMA CITY – St Andrews Street

1978- Open

The city's most recent cinema established as the local branch of the National Film Theatre. The 230 seat auditorium and ancillaries were formed within the Stuart and Suckling Halls and opened in April 1978 with a visit from Joseph Losey. It is an asset to be cherished, catering for every taste as a regular cinema while providing the showplace for specialist films.

SHERINGHAM
ELECTRIC PICTURE PALACE
– 36 Cromer Road

1914-1931 Change of use

Built by C.A. Sadler, a local businessman. Its facade followed a distinctive pattern of cinemas for this period and inside 400 patrons could be accommodated. May Ayers, in her "Memoirs of a Shannock" recalled her visits to this cinema. *"Often we paid one penny for a performance, sometimes threepence for the seats at the back, these were behind a velvet curtain which divided the better class seats, priced at ninepence, from the cheaper ones. Before we all went in we would buy bags of monkey nuts from a small grocer stall nearby. By the time we came out the floor would be carpeted with crushed and broken shells"*.

Sadler's, the proprietors, were well established business people in the town and their apprentice painter, Bob Gravelling, used to be sent up to the Electric to tear tickets on rainy days when he was unable to get on with his normal work. The Electric became the Casino in later years and was never wired for sound. During this time Mr Sadler sometimes found himself without films, so he shared reels with the cinema at Cromer. Young Norman Troller *(pictured on page 8)* would carry the films between cinemas on his motorcycle.

It closed in 1931 and became a shoe factory and more recently a Masonic Hall.

SHERINGHAM

THE REGENT – Cromer Road/Holway Road

1926-1960 Change of use

A few years before the Electric closed, C.A. Sadler built the Regent Hall which was home to the Sheringham Players and Operatic Society. It was a splendid theatre by all standards and became a cinema for the talkies with "Sunny Side Up" an early musical starring Janet Gaynor, produced in black and white film with a colour sequence. This film was so popular in the launch of talking pictures in this region that it was often referred to as "Money Side Up".

In 1938, the theatre was still advertised as the Regent Hall and boasted of its Duosonic Sound System. Its seating capacity was 600 in 1940 but had reduced to 534 seven years later. This often happened when cinemas were refurbished to create more legroom or to save tax on higher capacities.

In 1947 admission prices ranged from 10d (4p) to 2/9 (13p) with one show nightly and two on Saturday.

The cinema closed in December 1960 to become an auctioneer's saleroom and is now a snooker hall and ex-servicemen's club.

SHERINGHAM

Picture House/Empire – Station Road

1914-1960 Change of use

Silent films were shown on this site in what was then the Town Hall, a building dating from 1897.

By the coming of 'talking pictures' it was operating as The Picture House with 280 seats and utilising a 'sound on disc system'. Victor Harrison took the lease in 1930 and installed a new sound system to open with "Canaries Sometimes Sing".

Sadlers from the Regent ran it in 1958 with a name change to Empire.

It closed 30th April, 1960 and re-opened in July that year as The Little Theatre under the auspices of the local council. Since then it has been a successful seaside repertory theatre occasionally screening of films.

Some of the film seasons were operated by Colin Aldis from East Dereham as part of his CBA Cinemas venture during the 1960s.

STALHAM
THE BROADLAND – Brumstead Road
1955-1963 Change of use

This former 400 seat cinema was a brief but brave excursion into the business at a very uncertain time when cinemas were showing signs of closing. The Fisher family of Stalham, driven by enthusiasm and determination were granted permission to use the sounder parts of an old tithe barn to create the Broadland Cinema. They made their own concrete blocks, assembled the projection equipment from components bought in London and installed seats from an old theatre in Peterborough.

All was ready in time for a grand opening to show "A White Christmas" on 29th November, 1955.

The business was run by the entire family as efficiently as any cinema in a major circuit. It served the broads area for eight years before closing in September, 1963 and is serving as industrial premises.

SWAFFHAM

ELECTRIC PICTUREDROME/REGAL – 35 Station Street

1919-1964 Vacant

Swaffham's former cinema seen here camouflaged by nature, was established by Gaythorne Brearley from Brandon on the site of Mallan's joinery. At first it had a tin roof which made conversation impossible during heavy rain but was modernised after a fire in the 1920s.

In 1924 the interior was painted with an Egyptian mural by the local artist Harry Carter for a visit and lecture by his famous uncle, Howard Carter, the man who had gone first into the tomb of Tutankhamen.

Second-hand talking picture equipment was installed for the Picturedrome's first sound film "Atlantic" a story based on the Titanic disaster.

A name change to Regal came in 1936 when the cinema joined the Bostock circuit and on January 1st, 1937 it was proud to present the Charlie Chaplin epic film "Modern Times". At the time of the Coronation in 1953 the Regal was redecorated and announced itself as the "Best cinema in the district, with first-class sound and heating equipment".

Affectionate memories are recalled of women sitting in the front row with their knitting and of the man who came in on Saturday's to walk up and down the two aisles selling "The Pinkun" newspaper.

The decline brought eventual closure in 1964 and it later became a factory serving the catering industry.

THETFORD

PALACE – Guildhall Street

1913-1984 Change of use

This cinema opened as The People's Palace, built by one of the Barker family who had introduced moving pictures on the fairground. It flourished until the advent of "talking pictures" when the owner at the time saw no future in films that spoke with an American 'twang'. There was also competition from the Oddfellows Hall in Earles Street which operated during the first war as The Empire run by Walter Richard Stapely.

The People's Palace was bought in 1931 by Ben Culey who had been experiencing a depressing time as a farmer but was enamoured by the film business. He modernised the Thetford cinema, putting in new seating and projection equipment and cut short the name to "Palace". The present front was added by him and a later extension on the side.

Ben Culey was always concerned with providing good sound and picture and would sit in the audience occasionally to keep a check on quality. His devotion to the business paid dividends as he was able to keep The Palace open longer than most cinemas when the decline came. He even filmed his own local newsreels and screened them at the cinema. When the threat from television was at its height he installed a set in the foyer so that patrons could view the transmissions while queuing for the cinema.

For a while its survival was reliant on alternate nights of films and 'bingo' but since closure it remains another structure which has survived by the grace of the gaming craze.

WATTON

WAYLAND HALL – Market Place

1933-1937 Change of use

The Town Hall of 1835, a handsome building "in the late perpendicular style" had a large room on the upper floor for corn hall, assembly and concert use. This became Watton's first talking picture cinema on December 18th, 1933 with a presentation of "The Midshipmaid" with Jessie Matthews.

The sloping floor of the converted hall with proper tip-up cinema seats was reached by the existing stone staircase. The operation was managed in conjunction at one time with Mrs Yeates of Attleborough's cinema and continued in use until the opening of the modern Regal on Norwich Road.

WATTON
REGAL – Norwich Road
1937-1973 Change of use

This remains a classic example of the rural 'super' construction of the heyday of cinema design from J. Owen Bond of Norwich. It was built by Watton builders Peeke Vout and Sons for a local circuit, East Coast Cinemas and opened on February 8th, 1937.

The Regal's design was identical to that of the County at Aylsham and most of its accommodation has been put to practical use since closure in March 1973. The fabric has weathered well considering the original brief was that it should stand for just 25 years.

The building was used for storage and suffered a fire before its time as a workshop. Since 1982 it has been the storage depot for Richard Neave Ltd, Watton based removals, storage and shipping company.

WATTON

ELECTRIC CINEMA – Priory Road

1914-1932 Demolished

The 'silent' era in Watton was served by this wooden cinema in Hogg's Lane *(formerly Priory Road)*. Pictured here in 1972 as the local British Legion HQ it retains the small paybox on the right hand side. Joe Swann the projectionist operated from a compartment in the roof. The Electric closed when 'talkies' were presented in Wayland Hall.

WELLS

PARK CINEMA – Mill Road

1931-1937 Demolished

Cyril Claxton of Wells built this storage building then turned it into a cinema taking its name from Holkham Park, nearby. Herbert Wells from Hunstanton presented shows here, visiting with portable equipment. Later it came under the control of the Bostock Cinema Circuit.

106

WELLS

ELECTRIC/CENTRAL/REGAL – Clubbs Lane

1914-1973 Part demolished

The original cinema was created in the Oddfellows Hall shown here as the frontage to a larger, extended theatre. It was operated for some years as the Electric Palace in the 1920s by the Wells-next-the-Sea Cinema Syndicate. In 1931 it was operated and renamed The Central by Cyril Claxton who had built The Park in Mill Road.

Later it was gutted and revamped with the addition of a steel frame and rendered block auditorium to seat 310 patrons by East Coast Cinemas as part of the Bostock circuit and reopened as The Regal in December 1937. Like its sister cinema at Watton it was seen only as a 25 year project and came to a timely finish on March 31st, 1973.

The Regal remained vacant for a few years and in 1977 the local council considered its possible purchase as a community hall but the scheme fell through. In 1980 the auditorium was demolished leaving the 1885 Oddfellows Hall intact to be converted to a pair of dwellings, one being aptly named 'Regal Cottage'.

WYMONDHAM

PICTURE HOUSE – Town Green

1917-1940 Change of use

This was Wymondham's Town Hall built in 1888 where some of the earliest films were shown before it was transformed into The Picture House towards the end of the first war.

In 1926 the proprietor and general manager was A.E. Orton who ran one show nightly and three on Saturdays. The prices of admission then were sixpence (2.5p) and one and threepence (6p approx).

The Picture House was a successful enterprise through the 'silent era' to the 'talkies' until faced with the competition of a new luxury cinema, The Regal, built by the Bostock circuit in Friarscroft Lane. The proprietor at Town Green then was William Spalding and he managed to sustain his trade alongside the new rival. Indeed, his eventual closure was only implemented by being bought out by Bostock and he closed in 1940. This was proof that the continued presence of The Picture House would have been a threat to the Regal.

The building became the Anglo American Service Club in 1943 and later saw service as Photokraft's film processing plant. It is now an antique centre, snooker club and shops.

WYMONDHAM

REGAL – Friarscroft Lane

1937-1993 Change of use

Les King (left) the cinema's last manager was always proud to have maintained the Regal for longer than anyone had ever anticipated. He emerged with the kind of showmanship which has been present throughout cinema history.

In the mid 1930s Douglas Bostock, a descendant of the Bostock & Wombell Menagerie family bought the green field site with its convenient slope for the building of his new Wymondham cinema, a standard design of J. Owen Bond.

Thomas Gill & Son, by now experienced cinema builders, were well under way with the construction by February 1937.

The 503 seat Regal followed the familiar pattern of a steel frame infilled with hollow blocks rendered both sides.

On instruction from Mr Bostock it had to last no more than 25 years along with the others in his circuit spread from Essex to the Norfolk coast. Even today the architect is surprised that such places have survived in good order.

Almost 60 years ago there were no forebodings of a cinema closing as the Regal opened in a spectacular fashion on the evening of 18th March, 1937. Fred Astaire and Ginger Rogers shone from the screen in "Swing Time" which launched such songs as *"The way you look tonight"* and *"A fine romance"*.

The romance lasted almost to the day that Mr Bostock had predicted as the Regal closed on 17th June, 1962.

After standing derelict for two and a half years the cinema was bought by Norwich businessman, Roy Dashwood, who reopened 30th April, 1965 with "A Hard Days Night". Along with the show came Les King, employed to keep order during the films, which were often disrupted by rowdy youths. The position soon became permanent. He took over as manager in 1966 which led to his complete devotion in keeping the Regal open with himself as lessee in due course.

Les King was faced with all the frustrations of running what proved to be the most difficult cinema to maintain; its closeness to Norwich cinemas with competition from all the latest releases being available before he could secure them for Wymondham. Nevertheless he fought well with all manner of schemes and enticements to woe his patrons until the final curtain on 29th June, 1993.

The Regal is owned by the Wymondham Ex-Servicemen's Club and used for many functions.

(Page 112– the interior of The Regal)